# COMMON ANOMALY

# COMMON ANOMALY

*Business Basics*
*and Fundamentals For Teens*

Evan White

**To order additional copies of this book, contact:**
Xlibris LLC
1-888-795-4274
www.Xlibris.com
Orders@Xlibris.com
141350

# CONTENTS

# PART TWO

# Dedication

I dedicate this book to my dad for helping me every step of the way. When I first introduced the idea for this book, he encouraged me and took the time to read over numerous versions of the book. For something that seemed like a stretch for someone my age, he made my dream become a reality. To my mom, thanks for supporting everything I do including the writing of this book. To my first business class teacher, Mr. Dawson, along with the rest of the Eastern High School teachers and administrators, for showing me that something such as accounting, which I was sure I would not like, could be more fun and educational than I could have ever imagined. If not for all the support, this book would definitely not exist.

Thank You!

Shoutouts to: My brother Brandon, Em, Katya, Taryn, Zack, Jack, and especially Beau, who's been there for me from the start.

# Introduction

Money! Money makes the world go round. Money enables the poor man to afford his meal for the day and a rich man to buy that Lamborghini he has always wanted. The U.S. dollar is regulated and distributed throughout the United States by the government. Ultimately, the government watches over the fluctuating value of the dollar to ensure everything in the economy is in good condition. Now, you might be saying to yourself, "How does this relate to me?" Well, when you purchase your favorite bag of chips from your local grocer and you notice the price has gone up, this is usually because of all the decisions made during the typical business cycle to increase company profits and pass the additional operating cost on to you the consumer. The constant fluctuating value of the dollar impacts our investments here at home and when traveling abroad. Meaning, if the value of the U.S. dollar goes down, the U.S. dollar buys less in other countries raising the overall cost of international travel. For example, if you travel to Japan for vacation you may find that on the first day of your vacation, $100 of U.S. currency (after being converted to the Japanese Yen) can buy you a nice pair of shoes. However, if the value of the dollar fluctuates lower while you are on your vacation, the same $100 may not be enough to by the same exact pair of shoes forcing you to pay more. At any time you can go to *google.com* and type in the search term "how much is a dollar worth" to find out the value of a single U.S. dollar against other currencies in the world.

There's a lot that goes into making money, determining its value, spending money, and managing money. Regardless of where you work, you're paid money daily (every day), weekly (once a week), biweekly (every two weeks), monthly (once a month), etc. Money is managed in the workplace through basic functions such as paying employees, purchasing equipment, paying bills, and many other activities which are explained later in the book. Most people only talk about how the U.S. Federal Reserve prints money; the Federal Reserve also regulates the destruction of money. Yes, when money gets too old and torn, for example, the Federal Reserve takes money out of circulation by physically destroying old worn-out bills. Each type of U.S. bill has a specific life span of circulation:

- $1 bills: 3.7 years

- $5 bills: 3.4 years

- $10 bills: 3.4 years

- $20 bills: 5.1 years

- $50 bills: 12.6 years

- $100 bills: 8.9 years

In any given year, the Federal Reserve could destroy between $2 billion and $6 billion in physical cash.

## Letter to Teens: Getting Ahead

In general, *Common Anomaly* attempts to explain a number of the core components needed to understand and interpret the basic business concepts and financial breakdowns used in most businesses. Using basic examples, *Common Anomaly* also demonstrates how to apply what you learn as a future entrepreneur, as well as grasp a basic understanding of the ins and outs of Wall Street to affect your business. I am a highly motivated business-minded teen who understands the concept of getting ahead where my future is concerned. From giving presentations to executives at Sony in NYC to digging deep into what it means to calculate a Price Earnings (P/E) multiple for an acquisition based on extensive factors, I've most likely done it all. The primary reason I decided to write this book is to provide other teens with baseline knowledge to obtain a head start with understanding business in general with a little less complexity and a focus on keeping it simple. I believe this book will help strengthen any teen's knowledge by learning the basic concepts of business. I've been told by many adults who work in business and finance how much they would have benefited from learning the fundamentals of business earlier in their life.

Other than reading this book, there are many ways to get ahead. Taking business-oriented electives in high school will definitely help in understanding more advanced concepts as you read on your own and prepare for more advanced courses later. Applying for summer sessions and programs at colleges and universities for high school students interested in business, leadership, or any other related area can strengthen your skill set and could prove to be a valuable use of your time. In addition to acquiring an understanding of business concepts, it is equally important in today's business environment to have a sound understanding of Microsoft PowerPoint as a business tool. Also, asking questions to understand everything you're being introduced to is a way to truly grasp a firm understanding of the material being presented. Don't be afraid to raise your hand and ask questions because not doing so will leave you in the dark—unclear and confused.

Advancing your understanding of business as a teen can obviously be advantageous; however, it can be time consuming and shouldn't be a primary goal above and beyond your required studies for graduation. On a personal level, getting into my first college pick is important to me. I'm saying this to explain why I can't let reading an extra book on finance get in the way of studying for a microeconomics test or completing a school project. At sixteen, much of what I do in school and out of school is centered on becoming a more attractive candidate for colleges with the best business programs. However, while I do have my favorite colleges, I believe that in the end, I will only get out of any experience what I put into it. My suggestion is that everyone in high school approach college planning by first giving it one's all in high school and challenging oneself to become the best you can be as a student and member of the community.

# Part One

# Chapter One

## Overview

### What Is a Business?

A business is simply a person or a group of people that sell a good or service. Businesses are extremely profuse throughout the world. According to the Small Business Administration (SBA), in 2011, approximately 558,000 businesses were created each month in the United States. Anyone in the world can start a business especially if there's a particular need or demand for the product or service being provided to customers. For example, McDonald's provides quality food to the public in return for money. While it may seem like it's no big deal to order your food at the counter and swipe your card for payment, there is a lot that goes into the infrastructure of a business life cycle to create simplicity for consumers. But before we get into all the nitty-gritty details, let's talk about the various types of businesses you may see on a daily basis.

## Types of Businesses

There are four main types of businesses I would like to highlight. They are sole proprietorships, corporations, partnerships, and nonprofits. I'm going to explain the positives along with the negatives in starting up each of the four types of companies to provide you a good baseline going forward, either with your continued studies or as a young entrepreneur.

**Sole Proprietorship.** A Sole proprietorship is the easiest type of business to start. A Sole proprietorship is a type of business owned and maintained mainly by one person and requires no "legal" formation. There are no papers required to start a sole proprietorship which makes it so easy to create.

For example: If I were someone who had enough free time to use my lawn mower to go out and mow lawns for a certain price, I could start a business as a sole proprietorship company called "Fast Lawn Mowing" and make all my dreams a reality. Businesses such as personal fitness training, after-school tutoring, dog walking, and Mom & Pop house cleaning services are all examples of sole proprietorships.

Advantages

- Very easy to create
- Takes all the profits
- Easy to get rid of

Disadvantages

- Less revenue (money)
- Increased liability
- Greater personal risks

**Partnership.** A partnership is a type of business that does not require legal formation. A partnership must have two owners or shareholders. Any income obtained through the partnership is divided up between the partners at agreed percentages. There are different types of business taxes as partnerships, such as Limited Liability Corporations or LLCs. LLCs have mixed properties between partnerships and corporations (which I will explain later). They obtain flexibility and tax efficiencies of partnerships with limited liability features of a corporation.

For example: If I were still running Fast Lawn Mowing, I could ask my friend Bob to help trim the edge of the yards and form a partnership with me. To confirm the partnership, I'd have to create a written agreement outlining how the earnings and expenses will be divided up between Bob and me. A great example of a partnership is one of the biggest accounting firms in the world, Ernst & Young.

Advantages

-   Shared losses
-   More expertise
-   Increased resources (cash, assets, etc.)

Disadvantages

-   Joint decision making
-   Full liability (on each owner)
-   Shared profits

**Corporation.** Corporations, as a business type, are considered separate entities. Corporations have a type of limited liability for their shareholders (investors) and can also decide how much money to keep or spend. Forming a corporation involves a formal process with specific registrations. Depending on your level of involvement, legally forming a corporation can involve hiring an attorney, which can take a few weeks, or you can simply visit an online website and complete a few forms which may only take an hour. The corporation is my personal favorite because of the higher level of "personal" risk protection for everyone involved as seen with corporations such as Microsoft, Walmart, Google, and Apple, which are regularly challenged by the marketplace without the owners being "personally" liable in most situations.

For example: If my Fast Lawn Mowing company grew larger than expected, I could turn it into a corporation. Some things required for corporations are more owners/investors, a board of directors, and all the necessary legal documentation needed to consider my business a corporation.

Advantages

- Ability to gain capital through the selling of corporation stocks
- Asset ownership in company's name
- Limited liability for stockholders

Disadvantages

- More complex infrastructure (setup/management) requirements
- Enhanced government regulation
- Requires more overall governance

**Nonprofit Organizations (NPO).** NPOs are often referred to in the marketplace as "501(c)'s" which is in reference to the United States Internal Revenue Service's (IRS) designation code; they operate like businesses but have components unique to only nonprofits. Just like every other business, nonprofits have revenues and expenses; however, the revenue generated by a nonprofit must be used to sustain itself as well as for future expansion plans. The most important feature of a nonprofit organization is the "tax exempt" status. NPOs can be exempt from income and other taxes in the United States if they meet the requirements outlined by the IRS.

A great example of a nonprofit organization is the Ronald McDonald House for children. Its mission is to help give sick children's families a place to stay during their medical treatment. Donations are the primary source of revenue, but a lot of funding can come from McDonald's, which serves as a type of parent company to the Ronald McDonald House. In this situation, McDonald's Corporation pays taxes on its revenue, whereas the Ronald McDonald House is "exempt" from income taxes related to funds raised as an NPO.

# Chapter Two

## Basic Money Management

### Revenue

Accounting for the cash flow of a business is a core basic money management requirement. All the money that comes in through business operations is called "revenue." Revenue from my lawn mowing company, Fast Lawn Mowing, would be the money people paid me to mow their lawns. If I mowed 5 lawns a week for a year at a price of $10 per lawn, I would be generating revenue of about $2,600 annually (for the year).

$$5 \quad \text{x} \quad 10 \quad = \quad 50$$

(Lawns per Week)        (Dollars per Lawn)              (Dollars per Week)

$$50 \quad \text{x} \quad 52 \quad = \quad 2{,}600$$

(Dollars per Week)        (Weeks per Year)               (Annual Revenue)

The $2,600 I generated in revenue or gross income (income before taxes and expenses deducted) can be used, for example, to purchase more lawnmowers and hire more employees to grow the business. While growth is an option, first and foremost the first order of business is to pay the company's expenses.

## Expenses

Expenses are business costs generated while running your business. Expenses can sometimes be a tricky thing and come in many different shapes and forms. Every business has its own types of expenses it has to pay. Some of the expenses are standard and others may be unique to the business. Some general types of expenses that most businesses pay include:

- **Payroll**—when companies hire people, the expense that pays for how much each employee has earned (salary) is the payroll expense. Company payrolls are generally subject to various taxes that also have to be paid by the employees and employers (see Taxes).

- **Supplies**—supplies are a basic expense that again most companies have to pay. Items that would go under the supplies expense category include items such as pencils, pens, notebooks, paper, printer ink, etc.

- **Rent**—when businesses pay rent for the buildings where they conduct everyday business, the expense falls under an account called rent expense. Rent expenses usually vary when it comes to how often the rent expense is paid.

- **Advertising**—a good way for companies to get their names out there and circulated in public is through advertising. Using advertising to promote your brand can in effect increase revenue for whatever it is your business does. Basic forms of advertising include newspaper ads, billboard ads, and radio/television commercials.

- **Depreciation/Amortization**—depreciation/amortization is the lessening in value of long-term assets or resources over time. The difference between the two is physicality. The lessening in value of a long-term asset over time that *can* be touched is called depreciation. The lessening in value of a long-term asset over time that *cannot* be touched is called amortization. If I bought a lawn mower for $3,000 that I could only use for five years, this is what depreciation would look like:

## Straight Line Method

$$3,000 \quad / \quad 5 \quad = \quad 600$$

| (Starting Value of Lawn Mower) | (Years of Useful Life) | (Yearly Depreciation) |

| Year | Starting Value | Annual Depreciation | Accumulated Depreciation | Ending Value |
|------|---------------|---------------------|--------------------------|--------------|
| 1 | $3,000 | $600 | $600 | $2,400 |
| 2 | $2,400 | $600 | $1,200 | $1,800 |
| 3 | $1,800 | $600 | $1,800 | $1,200 |
| 4 | $1,200 | $600 | $2,400 | $600 |
| 5 | $600 | $600 | $3,000 | $0 |

There are many types of depreciation methods including declining balance method, sum-of-the-years' digits, and Modified Accelerated Cost Recovery System (MACRS). Amortization can be more difficult to calculate due to the dependencies on the type and usefulness of assets that can't be touched. Types of assets that can't be touched are trademarks, patents, and copyrights.

- Miscellaneous—an expense in the miscellaneous category would most likely be an expense that is a small amount and too specific to be put into any of the other expense categories. An example of a miscellaneous expense is a business meal.
- Taxes—business tax expenses are a particular expense paid regularly. Some taxes that businesses are often responsible for are federal income taxes, state income taxes, social security taxes, Medicare taxes, and unemployment taxes.

## Net Income

Net income is what is left when you subtract all the money you owe such as expenses, taxes, insurance, and employee benefits from the money you've made. Income can be used for many things in a company which is why companies try to increase net income. If net income is high enough in most companies, this means they can increase employee pay or improve working conditions and other benefits for employees. Net income also allows businesses to pay for various expenditures themselves without having to apply for loans and increasing their debt obligations. Net income gives companies the option to increase dividends to shareholders (which we'll learn about later in the book) or acquire other companies.

# Chapter Three

## The Balance Sheet

### Financial Statements

Documenting the activities of my lawn mowing business on a sheet of paper will highlight all the money I've made and how I've been spending the company funds. This type of financial documentation is known as the company's "Financial Statement." Financial statements are documents that help people understand how specific businesses are doing (thriving or dying) over a certain period of time. There are three main types of financial statements and they are the *balance sheet, income statement*, and *statement of cash flows.*

A company's balance sheet shows the *assets*, which are everything that the company owns (lawn mowers, lawn cutter, etc.); *liabilities*, which are everything that a company owes (loans, mortgages, etc.); and *owners' equity*, which is capital (financial investments) received from investors in exchange for ownership or stock.

# Assets = Liabilities + Owners' Equity

Now let's set up a little situation for each category to help explain how the balance sheet is actually used with Fast Lawn Mowing.

## Assets and Liabilities

If I borrow $10,000 from a bank, my assets would increase by $10,000 for the cash I received. However, because I borrowed the funds, my liabilities would also increase by $10,000. Here's a representation of what this transaction would look like on the balance sheet:

| Assets = | Liabilities + | Owners Equity |
|---|---|---|
| Cash | Money Owed to Bank | |
| +$10,000 | + $10,000 | |

## Assets and Owners' Equity

There's a section associated with owners' equity on the balance sheet called "retained earnings." Retained earnings are the accumulation or building up of net income over time. If I earned $9,000 from mowing lawns, then my assets are increased by $9,000, and my owners' equity is increased by $9,000. While this is what it would look like, another example that would look similar is someone buying stock in my company.

| Assets = | Liabilities + | Owners Equity |
|---|---|---|
| Cash | | Retained Earnings |
| +$9,000 | | +$9,000 |

## Asset Changes

In this case, one asset turns into another asset. If my Lawn Mowing company were to purchase another lawn mower for $2,500, then my assets would be deducted by $2,500 for the cash I paid, and my assets would increase by $2,500 for the lawn mower I received. This is what it would look like:

| Assets = | Liabilities + | Owners Equity |
|---|---|---|
| **Cash** <br> **−$2,500** <br> **Lawn Mower** <br> **+$2,500** | | |

# Part Two

Knowing how a company spends and manages its money is a great financial skill to have; however, having the expanded knowledge to perform basic evaluations on a company's financial health (strengths and weaknesses) is an even more powerful skill. Now, through the use of additional financial techniques, I will show you how you can gain valuable and beneficial insight about companies traded on various public exchanges.

# Chapter Four

## The Stock Market

When people are looking to invest in companies, they look at different components to determine the strengths and weaknesses of a company that can make or break a stock. Before any company can execute what is known as an "Initial Public Offering" (IPO) or sell a share of ownership, the company must first file an S1 Form with the U.S. Securities and Exchange Commission (SEC).

## IPO Rundown

IPOs are used to grow the value of a company through additional financial investments (new capital) from the public or business entities that are willing to invest. Usually when a company decides to go public, they are assisted by an investment bank to determine how many shares they want to sell, the types of shares, and how much they would be worth. Let's take the Facebook IPO as an example. Facebook was one of the biggest IPOs in history. On May 18, 2012, Facebook went public with an estimated valuation of over $100 billion with 3 billion shares outstanding. The people who helped them weigh the demand of their stock and create a price are called underwriters. Underwriters are companies or entities that administer help to the issuing bodies to closely determine offering price of the securities.

People usually have their personalized style of picking stocks. Some people lean toward quantitative indicators, indicators using mathematical or statistical techniques, while others lean more toward qualitative indicators, indicators that use subjective judgment to non-quantitative information. There are some technicals that can be used to determine the basic valuation of any company.

## Company Valuation Techniques

**Earnings Per Share.** Earnings per share can be calculated from the income statement. The earnings per share highlight how much money each individual outstanding stock earned over a certain time period. The more money that the company makes each year generally causes stocks to look more attractive because of the higher earnings per share.

$$\$100,000 \ / \ 40,000 = \$2.50$$

| (Net Income—Preferred Stock Dividends) | (Shares Outstanding) | (Earnings per Share) |

**Price Earnings (P/E) Ratio.** The P/E ratio is calculated using a stock market value, which is the value of a stock established by the buying and selling of a stock, and the earnings per share (calculated above). Different companies in different industries usually operate on a different average price earnings ratio. Typically the higher the P/E ratio, the better. Currently, Walmart's P/E ratio is 15 while Target, its competitor, has a P/E ratio of 16. While these aren't significantly different, this simply states that Target's investors are willing to pay $16 for every $1 of earnings as opposed to Walmart's investors who are only willing to pay $15. In summary, a good P/E ratio is 20 to 25 times earnings.

$$\$30 \quad / \quad \$2.50 \quad = \quad 12$$

<table>
<tr><td>(Market Share Price)</td><td>(Earning Per Share)</td><td>(Price Earnings Ratio)</td></tr>
</table>

Now, depending on the need for accounts receivables, this next ratio could be situational.

**Accounts Receivable Turnover Ratio.** The accounts receivable turnover ratio is calculated using net sales and the average accounts receivable. This ratio provides you the average number of days to collect a debt.

$$\$500,000 \quad / \quad \$80,000 \quad = \quad 6.3$$

<table>
<tr><td>(Net Credit Sales)</td><td>(Average Accounts Receivable)</td><td>(Turnover Ratio)</td></tr>
</table>

$$365 \quad / \quad 6.3 \quad = \quad 58$$

<table>
<tr><td>(Days in a Year)</td><td>(Turnover Ratio)</td><td>(Estimated Number of Days for Collection)</td></tr>
</table>

In general, the accounts receivable turnover ratio measures the efficiency of a business in collecting credit sales. Usually, a high ratio value in accounts receivable turnover is more favorable than a lower ratio value. A lower ratio value is usually an indication of a company's inefficiency in collecting outstanding sales (cash).

# Chapter Five

## Stocks

There is a lot of discussion about stocks in the news and some mention of stocks already in previous chapters of this book. In general, a stock is a portion of a company that represents partial ownership. There are two main types of stocks, common and preferred. Preferred stock is better because preferred stock owners generally receive higher dividends and have higher priority over common stocks. The downside with preferred stock is some preferred stocks do not come with voting rights where common stocks typically do. However, during the liquidation of a company, preferred stock owners will be paid out before common stock owners. Note, that these are not steadfast rules as they are customizable by each company.

## Dividends

Usually every quarter, more mature companies give their preferred and common stock owners a part of the company's earnings, referred to as dividends. Dividends consist of small amounts per share based on the company's performance usually calculated as a percentage of earnings.

$$\$100,000 \text{ X } 7\% = \$7,000$$

| (Quarterly Earnings) | (% for common stock dividends) | (Common Stock Dividends) |
|---|---|---|

$$\$7,000 \text{ / } 8,500 = \$0.82$$

| (Common Stock Dividends) | (Outstanding Common Stock) | (Dividends per Share) |
|---|---|---|

## Stock Splits

Stock splits are used by companies to decrease the value of shares if they become too "unattractive" or pricey for investors. When stock is split, there are more shares of that stock available, but the overall market value remains the same. Let's say I owned 100 shares of Fast Lawn Mowing at $50 per share. If the stock split was described as a two-for-one stock split, I would double my shares to 200 and decrease their value to $25. This is what it would look like.

**Pre-stock Split**    100 / $50 = $5,000

          (Shares of       (Market Value)       (Value of

          Fast Lawn                               Investment)

          Mowing)

**Post-stock Split**    200 / $25 = $5,000

          (Shares of         (Market         (Value of

          Fast Lawn           Value)          Investment)

          Mowing)

## Reverse Splits

If the stock split is reversed, you get a reverse split. A reverse split in this case would be a two for one transaction where 200 shares would be converted into 100 shares and the price would double. This causes the opposite outcome and raises the stock market price.

# Chapter Six

## Bonds

Fixed income securities, or bonds, are relatively long-term investments with a fixed schedule anywhere between one to thirty years. What separates bonds from stocks is that bonds pay a fixed amount of interest on a specific or recurring basis. Also, bonds repay you in full at the end of the bond's maturity date. The outlined risks of bonds include inflation, the value of the dollar going down, and defaulting, wherein the bond giver is unable to make interest and/or maturity payments on time.

## Corporate

When companies need money to fund different projects, expand their company, or acquire other companies, they may use bonds to aid this process. The risk with bonds usually runs higher than government bonds, but generally where there is more risk, there is more reward.

## Government

Bonds issued by the government are most often referred to as treasury bonds. Treasury bonds are backed by the assurance of the U.S. government. Treasury bonds basically guarantee your money back with earnings as long as other factors such as inflation or rising interest rates, which are directly related, do not reduce returns.

## Municipal

Municipal bonds are financial obligations that states, counties, cities, and townships use when they need money to fund various projects such as new roads, parks, and schools. Municipal bonds can be taxed or tax-free. However, since tax-free bonds generate income for the investor, they tend to get most of the attention.

# Chapter Seven

# Hybrids

When it comes to investing, people have the choice of investing in stock based equity securities or debt based government bond securities where you're paid a fixed amount over time. With hybrid securities or "hybrids," you get both equity and debt characteristics.

## Options

Options are unique types of financial options contracts called "puts" and "calls" that are mainly tools of speculation. An option gives you the right, but not the obligation, to buy shares of a company at a price higher or lower than what it currently commands at a later time. The concept can be difficult to grasp, but once it clicks, you realize how useful it can be and the amount of risk it assumes.

## Types of Options

**Calls**—A call option provide the owner (buyer) the option to purchase a stock at a specific "strike" price during a specific window of time in the future. If the call option is not exercised before the specified date, the call option will expire.

**Puts**—A put option provides the owner (seller) the option to sell a stock at a specific "strike" price during a specific window of time in the future. If the put option is not exercised before the specified date, the put option will expire.

## Futures

Similar to options, futures are a type of option that obligates you to buy instead of giving you the right to buy. Futures can be set up to buy assets including cash or a physical asset such as gold. If I was a business looking to buy an asset worth $5 that was fluctuating too quickly in price and I wanted to lock it in at $5, I would buy a futures contract with the supplier. The terms would be that if the price of the asset increases, the seller assumes the cost over $5, and if the price goes lower than $5, he assumes the profit between the price and $5. The situation is vice versa for the buyer.

It is important to note that futures are a type of stock/options "contract". Each year, these stock index futures, stock index options, and stock options expire at a time which has come to be known as the "triple witching hour". Triple witching hour is the final hour of the stock market trading session on the third Friday of every March, June, September, and December. When all three contracts expire at once, market traders rush to balance portfolios that can trigger significant volatility in the markets. During triple witching, computerized trading goes into overdrive with traders trying to balance portfolios to ensure they are not exposed to massive losses should the markets not move in their favor.

# Chapter Eight

## Modern Money

### Currency in an Evolving World

Imagine a world where you could go to a store, take out your phone, and buy food with virtual currency not associated with the value of U.S. currency. Well if you don't already know, it's actually possible. Virtual currency is a currency not connected in any way to the value of the U.S. dollar or any other international currency. Virtual currency, such as the "Bitcoin," is evaluated based on its scarcity to obtain, as well as, how widely accepted it is in the virtual marketplace. Because of its rarity, by the time this book is published, each virtual Bitcoin will have an estimated value of $103.90 real U.S. dollars. Meaning, if you were to go to some restaurants that accept Bitcoins you could buy real world meals and services.

The logic and process for determining the actual "dollar value" of a bit coin is extremely confusing and a bit ridiculous, yet somehow virtual coins are being converted in to real dollars. This new currency has triggered the monitoring attention of the U.S. Department of Treasury and the IRS. Recently, the use of Bitcoins was connected to illicit activities and money laundering. My suggestion is to stay away from virtual currencies attempting to operate in the real world as cash. Virtual coins used in video games and smartphone games to enhance game play are a different type of virtual coin and are still safe to use.

## Recreating the Startup: Innovation within Fundraising

When new startup companies have what they think is a great new idea, they need money to finance that idea. Now one day in the future, I hope to be a venture capitalist investing in new ideas; however, if I was to start a business now, I would use an innovative funding technique used by many today called crowd funding. Crowd funding is when certain individuals pitch their ideas to a large number of people and these people invest a certain amount of money to a pool that eventually will be used to build or develop the product and bring it to the market. If you're a teen with a good idea and want to bring your idea to market, look no further than websites such as Kickstarter, Razoo, or Crowdfunder. Crowd funding websites allow people to present their ideas to the public, and if the public think it's a good idea, they invest through donations toward the idea. Since the launch of crowd funding websites, as much as $16 million has been raised for a single effort, and all business types use this new funding option including nonprofit organizations. If you are a young filmmaker, you can even use crowd funding to raise money to bring your film to market. Two possible downsides to crowd funding websites is that first, the people who invest can't gain a financial benefit in the future, and second, when you post your idea, you open the door for someone to steal your concept or challenge you in the marketplace. The core reason someone would invest is to bring to the market a product they believe in.

A possible upside to investing in Kickstarter opportunities is you can help bring to market a product you have serious interest in "and" be one of the first to obtain the product fresh off the manufacturing line. For those trying to launch a new business through Kickstarter, one key benefit is raising the money you need without having to give anyone a share of your company or having to pay them back. Crowd funding sites also provide you a list of people interested in buying your product once you bring it to market.

# Closing Comments

Learning about business is a skill that many people can benefit from even if starting a business is not the ultimate goal. While this book has hopefully given you a well-rounded insight on how businesses work, there's a lot more to learn. It would be a good idea to keep this book as a reference if you need assistance with remembering a couple of vocabulary terms or valuation techniques. I look forward to the many aspects of business left to learn, and as I continue my studies, I encourage every teen to learn as much as he or she can and take the business world by storm. As millennials we should take advantage of the many changes in the business world and become a part of the process in creating jobs domestically and internationally.

Good luck!

www.ingramcontent.com/pod-product-compliance
Lightning Source LLC
Chambersburg PA
CBHW021043180526
45163CB00005B/2254